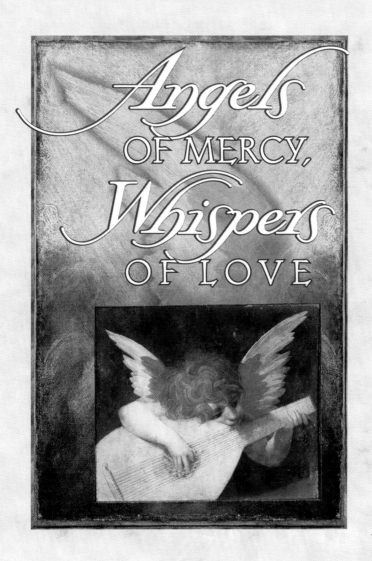

Angels
OF MERCY,
Whispers
OF LOVE

ISBN 1-57051-002-4

Cover/interior: Koechel Peterson & Associates

Printed in USA

A Special Gift

For

_____

From

_____

Date

_____

Angels
OF MERCY,
Whispers
OF LOVE

Edited by Paul C. Brownlow

BROWNLOW PUBLISHING COMPANY

∾ BROWNLOW GIFT BOOKS ∾

❧ Contents ❧

CHAPTER ONE

I Want to Be an Angel

For thousands of years we have been captivated and intrigued by the subject of angels, and so our current fascination with them should be no surprise. Angels are radiant creatures endowed with splendor and shrouded in mystery. And the popular myth (that we will become angels when we die) continues to excite us. A poet expressed it quite simply for some of us:

> I want to be an angel,
> And with the angels stand.
> A crown upon my forehead,
> A harp within my hand.
>
> URANIA BAILEY

While we are not now angels and will not become angels when we die, we can nevertheless carry out, in a limited way, the work and mission of angels. We can "be an angel" so to speak by doing what angels do, by learning to live as the angels live, to love as the angels love.

Angels were created by God to serve those who are heirs of salvation, the saints on earth. Think of it—God created a special class of beings just to serve our needs, to minister to our lives. This act alone should forever prove His wonderful love for us. This alone, without remembering the ultimate expression of His love in Jesus, should remind us that we are exalted, cared for, and most loved.

But the service of angels in our behalf is not optional; it is not just when convenient; it is not just an activity for some angels who desire it. The Bible states it in the most forceful manner:

> *Are not all angels ministering spirits sent*
> *to serve those who will inherit salvation?*
> HEBREWS 1:14

Thus we are assured that *all* angels are engaged in all-consuming service for the benefit of those who love God. Angels are not directing their own destinies or controlling their own choices of service. They are sent by God and are entirely under His control.

If a special class of heavenly beings, that is superior to mankind, has been created just to serve, what then do we learn of the ministry of service? To serve others is not too lowly, too far beneath our talents, or too humble for our gifts. The Son of God came to serve. Angels were created to serve. And we too must see the beauty and glory of service. To serve is to be like God. To serve is to be like angels.

How exactly angels serve God's people today, we simply are not told. But we do have a partial record of their past activities and interests for us to emulate:

∾ *Angels proclaimed the good news of Jesus' coming, His birth and His resurrection.* Angels rejoice when just one sinner comes home to God. The good news of Jesus is still good news, and is still unknown by many. We can continue to proclaim it and rejoice in its acceptance.

*A*ngels were created by God to serve
those who are heirs of salvation,
the saints on earth.

Angels rescued Lot from Sodom and delivered the apostles from prison. Are there not those around us to be delivered from the enslavements and enticements of our modern-day Sodoms? Are there not souls to be rescued from the private prisons of addiction, from the dungeons of self-abasement?

Angels were sent to strengthen Jesus in Gethsemane during His hour of temptation. We are surrounded today by friends, loved ones and family who are in the trials of temptation and who need our help.

Angels closed the mouths of lions for Daniel and fire-proofed the trio of young Hebrews. Can we not find faithful ones among us to support, comfort and protect from the perils of this life?

Angels attended the empty tomb of Jesus and comforted the bereaved. The bereaved, like the poor, we will have with us always, and thus the ministry of comforting the bereaved is ever before us.

Angels spoke a word of hope and encouragement to the Apostle Paul after the trauma of his shipwreck. We all sail in a sea of shipwrecked souls needing a word of direction, encouragement and hope.

So if we really want to live and love as the angels, we are surrounded by opportunities. We must forego the crown and harp, and submit our lives totally under God, in His service, for the benefit of His people. We must rediscover the beauty of service.

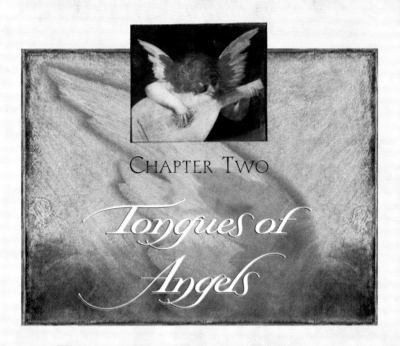

CHAPTER TWO

Tongues of Angels

In this dim world of clouding cares,
  We rarely know, till 'wildered eyes
  See white wings lessening up the skies,
The angels with us unawares.

GERALD MASSEY

Hold the fleet angel fast until he bless thee.

NATHANIEL COTTON

The angel of the LORD encamps around those
who fear him, and he delivers them.

PSALM 34:7

Angels we have heard on high
Singing sweetly through the night,
And the mountains in reply
Echoing their brave delight.

FRENCH CHRISTMAS CAROL

Every breath of air and ray of light and heat,
every beautiful prospect, is, as it were,
the skirts of their garments, the weaving of
the robes of those whose faces see God.

JOHN HENRY NEWMAN

To comfort and to bless,
    To find a balm for woe,
To tend the lone and fatherless,
    Is angels' work below.

W. W. HOW

Matthew, Mark, Luke, and John,
The bed be blest that I lie on.
Four angels to my bed,
Four angels round my head,
One to watch, and one to pray,
And two to bear my soul away.

THOMAS ADY

Although I'm Not an Angel

So, although I'm not an angel,
* yet I know that over there*

I will join the blessed chorus
* that the angels cannot share;*

I will sing about my Saviour,
* who upon dark Calvary*

Freely pardoned my transgressions,
* died to set a sinner free.*

JOHNSON OATMAN

Sleep on in peace, await thy Maker's will,
Then rise unchanged, and be an Angel still.

EPITAPH ON THE TOMB OF MARY ANGELL,
NOTTINGHAM, ENGLAND

Praise God, ye heavenly host above;
Praise Him, all creatures of His love.

A. H. D. TROYTE

For fools rush in where angels fear to tread.

ALEXANDER POPE

The angels keep their ancient places; –
Turn but a stone, and start a wing!

FRANCIS THOMPSON

Tongues of Men and Angels

If I speak in the tongues of men and of angels,
but have not love, I am only a resounding gong
or a clanging cymbal. If I have the gift of
prophecy and can fathom all mysteries and
all knowledge, and if I have a faith that can
move mountains, but have not love,
I am nothing. If I give all I possess to the poor
and surrender my body to the flames,
but have not love, I gain nothing.

1 CORINTHIANS 13:1-3

Writ in the climate of heaven,
in the language spoken by angels.

HENRY WADSWORTH LONGFELLOW

To love for the sake of being loved is human, but
to love for the sake of loving is angelic.

ALPHONSE DE LAMARTINE

But all God's angels come to us disguised:
Sorrow and sickness, poverty and death,
One after another lift their frowning masks,
And we behold the Seraph's face beneath,
All radiant with the glory and the calm
Of having looked upon the front of God.

JAMES RUSSELL LOWELL

Golden harps are sounding,
Angel voices ring,
Pearly gates are opened,
Opened for the King.

FRANCES R. HAVERGAL

At that time men will see the Son of Man coming
in clouds with great power and glory. And he will
send his angels and gather his elect from the four
winds, from the ends of the earth to the ends of
the heavens.

MARK 13:26-27

Remember though thy foes
are strong and tried,
The angels of Heaven
are on thy side,
and God is over all!

ADELAIDE ANNE PROCTER

CHAPTER THREE

Whispers of Love

So much is included in this one word—love. Everything that is good and beneficial. It is the highest and worthiest virtue. It has no equal. This is why God is called *love.* Thus the inference is clear—the more love we have, the more godly we will be.

Love's superiority is also seen in that the Two Great Commandments are based on love:

> *Thou shalt love the Lord thy God*
> *With all thy heart,*
> *And with all thy soul,*
> *And with all thy mind.*
> *This is the first and great commandment.*

And the second is like unto it,
Thou shalt love thy neighbor as thyself.
MATTHEW 22:37-39

Since the greatest commandments are founded on love, then it follows that love must be the greatest of all attributes.

Love is so all-inclusive and all-embracing of compounded goodness that the Apostle Paul put it ahead of even faith and hope. He declared:

But now abideth faith, hope, love, these three;
and the greatest of these is love.
1 CORINTHIANS 13:13

Why? Because where there is love, there is faith and there is hope. So love is greater than either, for the whole is always greater than its parts. Just like the foot is greater than its toes, and the hand is greater than its fingers.

This is why the person with a loving heart—no hate, no bitterness, no resentment—excels all the rest and attains the highest peak of living.

Ah, how skillful grows the hand
That obeyed Love's command!
And he who followeth Love's behest
Far excelleth all the rest.
HENRY WADSWORTH LONGFELLOW

❧ *The world's most effective transforming power is love.* It is the lofty force that could cure the many ills in our society: Ills in religion because love has taken a back pew or moved out entirely. Ills in business because love has been replaced by greed. Ills in society because of misplaced love—love of self rather than the other person. Ills in family life because love has lost its dominance and self-ishness has lifted its head. Indeed, the unfailing cure for self-interest is love. For love "seeketh not her own."

In a farm family in which death took both parents in a short time, five children were left to make their own way. The eldest was a girl eighteen years of age who was determined to keep the orphan family together. On her rested the responsibility of being both mother and father to the young ones. Work! Work! Work! She had to work from early morning until late at night: plowing, planting, harvesting, gardening, milking, canning, cooking, sewing, laundering and the doing of a hundred other things. In time, it broke her health; she developed tuberculosis where it finally reached its last stages. Realizing that life was gradually ebbing away, she said to the minister who often visited her, "I know it won't be long until I reach the end and it seems I've done so little in life. I don't know what I'm going to tell the Lord for not doing more." The preacher said, "Don't tell Him anything. Just show Him your hands."

Those were unselfish hands. The hands of love. A love so great that it had completely forgotten self.

Instead of self-centeredly seeking to get, to exploit and to take advantage of others, love—unselfish love—gives and gives and gives. For this is love's way.

> *Love ever gives—*
> *Forgives—outlives—*
> > *And ever stands*
> > *With open hands.*
> > *And while it lives—*
> *It gives*
> > *For this is love's prerogative—*
> > *To give—and give—and give.*
> > JOHN OXENHAM

Yes, definitely, one of love's most appreciated attributes is its unselfish, sacrificial nature. It will live and die for its love. And in the latter instance, it is love at its fullest. For there is no more selfless gift than one's own life. The Bible holds this maxim before us: "Greater love hath no man than this, that a man lay down his life for his friends" (John 15:13).

∾ Since love is a decision regulated by the lover, not the one being loved, then it is possible for one to love everybody, even enemies. Actually, it is more than a possibility; it is a definite command given by Jesus:

But I say unto you,
Love your enemies,
Bless them that curse you,
Do good to them that hate you,
And pray for them which despitefully
  use you and persecute you.
MATTHEW 5:44

Obedience to this command is within the reach of all, because love is a feeling that manifests itself in keeping with who we are, not what the other person is. That is why God loves everyone—not that everyone is lovable. Hence, we see that it is not unreasonable to love an enemy. And the more we do it, the more we are changed into the likeness of God.

From both the Biblical and philosophical viewpoints we see the wisdom of loving our enemies. Meeting enmity with enmity aggravates and multiplies the problem. Hating them back brings only more hate and strife and heartbreak. Since like begets like and reaping depends on sowing, then there is a chance that loving an enemy may break through that hard, calloused crust of ill will and convert it into love, and thereby change the order of events. Maybe not. But it can. For the principle of reciprocal love is an accepted fact and is stated in the Bible:

We love him, because he first loved us.
1 JOHN 4:19

But if we should not be able to love the animosity out of an enemy, we still have triumphed; we have won over a lower inclination and have become better for having tried. And happier. Because there is a greater blessing in loving than in being loved. This being true, remember—there is no wasted love.

> Talk not of wasted affection,
>   affection never was wasted;
> If it enrich not the heart of another,
>   its waters, returning
> Back to their springs, like the rain,
>   Shall fill them full of refreshment.
>
> HENRY WADSWORTH LONGFELLOW

It is not trite, therefore, to say that love will solve our problems, no more stereotyped than to say that food sustains life. Without food we die; and without love we die a death worse than physical. The reason—we are creatures in need of love. Our hearts cry out for affection, affection to give and affection to receive. We need to love and we need to be loved. Nothing will adequately take its place.

> Better is a dinner of herbs where love is, than a stalled ox and hatred within.
>
> PROVERBS 15:17

Let us, therefore, never doubt the efficacy and utility of love.

Doubt, if you will, the being who loves you,
Woman or dog, but never doubt love itself.

ALFRED DE MUSSET

༅ *Now let us bear in mind that love — this beautiful quality — is available to all* if all will open their hearts to God and allow it to grow. It is not the exclusive property of the educated nor the wealthy nor the prestigious. It does not have to come in a luxury package. Neither does it have to be wrapped in a college diploma. It is something each, regardless of station in life, can speak and demonstrate in his or her own way; and, after all, that simple heart language is the most beautiful poetry and the grandest eloquence. Love is simple. And its power and joy are the same in all.

LEROY BROWNLOW

CHAPTER FOUR

From Realms of Glory

The Touch of the Angel's Hand

Life is so generous a giver, but we,
Judging its gifts by their covering,
Cast them away as ugly, or heavy, or hard.
Remove the covering, and you will
 find beneath it,
A living splendor, woven of love,
 by wisdom, with power.
Welcome it, grasp it, and you touch the
Angel's hand that brings it to you.
Everything we call a trial, a sorrow, or a duty,
Believe me, that angel's hand is there.

FRA GIOVANNI

The Angel's Song

It came upon the midnight clear,
  The glorious song of old,
From Angels bending near the earth
  To touch their harps of gold;
"Peace on the earth, good will to men
  From Heaven's all gracious King."
The world in solemn stillness lay
  To hear the angels sing.

EDMUND HAMILTON SEARS

How sweetly did they float upon the wings
Of silence through the empty-vaulted night,
At every fall smoothing the raven down
Of darkness till it smiled!

JOHN MILTON

Cherubim, seraphim, all the angelic host as they
are described in Scripture, have a wild and radiant
power that often takes us by surprise. They are not
always gentle. They bar the entrance to Eden, so
that we may never return home. They send
plagues upon the Egyptians. They are messengers
of God. They are winds. They are flames of fire.
They are young men dressed in white.

MADELEINE L'ENGLE

The Night the Angels Sang

GLORIA

And there were shepherds living out in the fields nearby, keeping watch over their flocks at night. An angel of the Lord appeared to them, and the glory of the Lord shone around them, and they were terrified. But the angel said to them, "Do not be afraid. I bring you good news of great joy that will be for all the people. Today in the town of David a Savior has been born to you; he is Christ the Lord. This will be a sign to you: You will find a baby wrapped in cloths and lying in a manger."

Suddenly a great company of the heavenly host appeared with the angel, praising God and saying,

> *"Glory to God in the highest,*
> *and on earth peace to men on*
> *whom his favor rests."*

When the angels had left them and gone into heaven, the shepherds said to one another, "Let's go to Bethlehem and see this thing that has happened, which the Lord has told us about."

So they hurried off and found Mary and Joseph, and the baby, who was lying in the manger. When they had seen him, they spread the word concerning what had been told them about this child, and all who heard it were amazed at what the shepherds said to them. But Mary treasured up all these things and pondered them in her heart. The shepherds returned, glorifying and praising God for all the things they had heard and seen, which were just as they had been told.

LUKE 2:8-20

From Realms of Glory

If the angelic image of Jesus has been impressed deeply enough on our hearts, some of the halo of his glory will be seen on our faces. As it was with Stephen (Acts 6:15), so it will be with us.

JAMES SMITH

What know we of the Blest above
But that they sing, and that they love?

WILLIAM WORDSWORTH

And with the morn those angel faces smile
Which I have loved long since, and lost awhile.

JOHN HENRY NEWMAN

See, I am sending an angel ahead of you to guard you along the way and to bring you to the place I have prepared. Pay attention to him and listen to what he says. Do not rebel against him; he will not forgive your rebellion, since my Name is in him.

EXODUS 23:20-21

The angels all were singing out of tune,
    And hoarse with having little else to do,
Excepting to wind up the sun and moon,
    Or curb a runaway young star or two.

LORD BYRON

The stars shine on brightly while Adam and Eve pursue their way into the far wilderness. There is a sound through the silence, as of the falling tears of an angel.

ELIZABETH BARRETT BROWNING

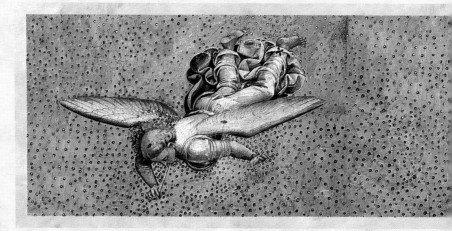

Millions of spiritual creatures walk the earth Unseen, both when we wake,
   and when we sleep:
All these with ceaseless praise
   his works behold
Both day and night.

JOHN MILTON

Thou hast the sweetest face I ever look'd on. Sir, as I have a soul, she is an angel.

WILLIAM SHAKESPEARE

Man is neither angel nor beast; and the misfortune
is that he who would act the angel acts the beast.

BLAISE PASCAL

Come, let us join our cheerful songs
With angels round the throne;
Ten thousand thousand are their tongues,
But all their joys are one.

ISAAC WATTS

The earth is to the sun what man is to the angels.

VICTOR HUGO

And yet, as angels in some brighter dreams
Call to the soul when man doth sleep,
So some strange thoughts transcend our
  wonted themes,
And into glory peep.

HENRY VAUGHAN

Silently one by one, in the infinite
  meadows of heaven
Blossomed the lovely stars,
  the forget-me-nots of the angels.

HENRY WADSWORTH LONGFELLOW

CHAPTER FIVE

Angels Unaware – The Gift of Hospitality

*W*hile love is the new commandment of Jesus to his disciples, and is described as the sum of the Divine Law and the greatest of the virtues, we are not left with only broad, ambiguous generalities. God is practical, and thus shows us *how* to manifest love in the detailed duties and difficulties of daily life.

  One way for us to show love is to demonstrate our ready and cheerful hospitality:

> *Be not forgetful to entertain strangers: for thereby some have entertained angels unawares.*
> HEBREWS 13:2

While we are to love one another, the stranger—as well as the brother—must have a place in our hearts. Brotherliness must not lead to exclusiveness.

However, we are quick to plead our inadequacies—that our homes are too small and our resources too feeble. To such ready objections, God would remind us that hospitality is not dependent upon sumptuous banquets or palatial homes. Hospitality is the genuine sharing of our blessings, whether large or small. Hospitality is the ability to use what we have to bless others. In a very pointed parable, Jesus reminded us that those who are faithful in using what they have, large or small, will be rewarded accordingly.

∿ *So what does it matter if we have very little of this world's goods.* Whatever it is, it has been given to us by God. Shall the lark refuse to chirp its melody because he cannot pour forth the luscious notes of the nightingale? Shall the robin refuse to sing merrily in the winter because he cannot undertake the long flight of the swallow? Shall the violet withhold its fragrance because the sunflower is so conspicuously larger? In the same way, we must use the gifts we are given for the benefit and blessing of others. God regards quality rather than quantity.

Let the stranger be ever in our minds. Let no one slip past our gates, or go away knocking in vain. We are called to an unremitting watchfulness in hospitality. What will it avail to admit a thousand who bring nothing but their needs, if we let the one go away who will bring us blessings far greater than anything we can do for him?

Many a guest has proved as an angel to his hosts, brightening the home by his presence, and leaving behind him precious memories and saving influences. The kindness we have shown to strangers will ultimately journey back to us with compound interest, and in higher and holier forms. As Jesus said, "Inasmuch as ye have done it unto one of the least of these my brethren, ye have done it unto me."

C. JERDAN

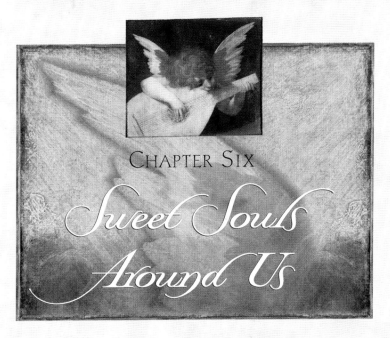

CHAPTER SIX

Sweet Souls Around Us

I, too, would seek the angels to follow,
Lord of all angels, wilt Thou me hallow?
I fain would emulate their holy zeal,
I fain would their glad obedience feel,
My forehead, like theirs, Thy holiness seal.

ANONYMOUS

Around our pillows golden ladders rise,
And up and down the skies,
With winged sandals shod,
The angels come, and go, the Messengers of God!

RICHARD HENRY STODDARD

When angels come, the devils leave.

PROVERB

The angels may have wider spheres of action
and nobler forms of duty than ourselves,
but truth and right to them and to us are one
and the same thing.

EDWIN HUBBELL CHAPIN

If instead of a gem, or even a flower, we should
cast the gift of a loving thought into the heart of a
friend, that would be giving as the angels give.

GEORGE MACDONALD

But you have come to Mount Zion, to the heavenly
Jerusalem, the city of the living God. You have
come to thousands upon thousands of angels in
joyful assembly, to the church of the firstborn,
whose names are written in heaven.

HEBREWS 12:22-23

Sweet souls around us watch us still,
   Press nearer to our side;
Into our thoughts, into our prayers,
   With gentle helpings glide.

HARRIET BEECHER STOWE

She Folds Her Wings

She doeth little kindnesses
Which most leave undone or despise;
For naught that sets one heart at ease,
And giveth happiness or peace,
Is low-esteemed in her eyes.

She hath no scorn of common things;
And, though she seem of other birth,
Round us her heart entwines and clings,
And patiently she folds her wings
To tread the humble paths of earth.

JAMES RUSSELL LOWELL

Angels from friendship
gather half their joy.

EDWARD YOUNG

An angel stood and met my gaze,
Through the low doorway of my tent;
The tent is struck, the vision stays; —
I only know she came and went.

JAMES RUSSELL LOWELL

Angels see only the light,
and devils only the darkness.

JAKOB BÖHME

Speak ye who best can tell,
  ye sons of light,
Angels, for ye behold him,
  and with songs
And choral symphonies,
  day without night,
Circle his throne rejoicing.

JOHN MILTON

Angels, as 'tis but seldom
  they appear,
So neither do they make
  a long stay;
They do but visit and away.

JOHN NORRIS

Holy Angels Bright

Ye holy angels bright
Who wait at God's right hand,
Or through the realms of light
Fly at your Lord's command,
Assist our song,
Or else the theme
Too high doth seem
For mortal tongue.

JOHN HAMPDEN GURNEY

Praise the Lord, you his angels,
  you mighty ones who do his bidding,
  who obey his word.
Praise the Lord, all his heavenly hosts,
  you his servants who do his will.

PSALM 103:20-21

It was pride that changed angels into devils; it is humility that makes men as angels.

AUGUSTINE

To equip a dull, respectable person with wings would be but to make a parody of an angel.

ROBERT LOUIS STEVENSON

And the wearied heart grows strong,
  As an angel strengthened him,
  Fainting in the garden dim
'Neath the world's vast woe and wrong.

JOHANN RIST

Angels from the realms of glory,
  Wing your flight o'er all the earth;
Ye, who sang creation's story,
  Now proclaim Messiah's birth.

JAMES MONTGOMERY

CHAPTER SEVEN

Fountains of Gladness

Our world is hard enough without the ruffles caused by the sour, unhappy, unkind individual; we have enough troubles without the commotions created by the cold, cruel person. A little kindness makes a big difference, and brings great joy to all of us.

> *A kind heart is a fountain of gladness, making*
> *everything in its vicinity freshen into smiles.*
> WASHINGTON IRVING

➳ ***It is truly a delight to be with the mild and calm person;*** and inasmuch as like begets like, the same spirit rubs off on others. Indeed, kind associates are what we all need. Give me the considerate look! The gentle voice!

The kind hand! I need it. Furthermore, I respond more graciously to good treatment. And, generally speaking, so does the other person. And as my path crosses his and my words meet his, may I keep this in mind and treat him respectfully and kindly. He is apt to pass it on, at least a little of it. And that is what the world needs.

> *Have you had a kindness shown?*
> > *Pass it on.*
> *It was not given to you alone,*
> > *Pass it on.*
> *Let it travel through the years;*
> *Let it wipe another's tears;*
> *Till in heaven the deed appears,*
> > *Pass it on.*

If we are never kind to others, what good are we in the world? None! No good to self, no good to our fellowman. Life is only a vain existence. However —

> *If by one word I help another,*
> *A struggling and despairing brother,*
> > *Or ease one bed of pain;*
> *If I but aid some sad one weeping,*
> *Or comfort one, lone vigil keeping,*
> > *I have not lived in vain.*

Moreover, the unkind life is more than vain; it is waste, wasted living. For that person misses the happiest and more profitable part of living. The gentle acts of kindness and love will live on forever—in another life and maybe on another shore.

Kindness Lives Forever

Kind words can never die;
  Cherished and blest,
God knows how deep they lie
  Stored in the breast,
Like childhood's simple rhymes,
Said o'er a thousand times,
Aye, in all lands and climes
  Distant and near.

Sweet thoughts can never die,
  Though, like the flowers,
Their brightest hues may fly
  In wintry hours;
But when the gentle dew
Gives them their charm anew,
With many an added hue
  They bloom again.

AUTHOR UNKNOWN

❧ *Kindness is a pleasing and powerful sermon in practice* — one no one misunderstands. Even the deaf can hear and the blind can see kindness. The Four Gospels we commonly speak of are Matthew, Mark, Luke and John, and the fifth is kindness. Those who never read nor hear the four can be swayed by the fifth, for it is very visible and exceedingly audible. It unmistakably comes through clearly and persuasively. This we see from Peter's exposition of the topic:

> *If any obey not the word, they [husbands] also may without the word be won by the conversation [conduct] of their wives.*
>
> 1 PETER 3:1

❧ *It is obvious that an urgent need* in this world of ours that has turned insensitive to the wants of others is to *show a heart.* For it takes a heart to win a heart. I am inclined to believe what Henry Ward Beecher said: "Though the world needs reproof and correction, it needs kindness more; though it needs the grasp of the strong hand, it needs, too, the open palm of love and tenderness."

❧ *Maybe some of our unkindness is due to a failure to think.* I am not trying to excuse any of us, just trying to be realistic and fair, but maybe some of our unkindness is due to a failure to think. "I wasn't thinking" is an often belated expression of our rough manners. The hurt, nevertheless, was done and a heart was wounded.

To comfort and to bless,
To find a balm for woe,
To tend the lone and fatherless,
Is angels' work below.

W.W. HOW

The wounds I might have healed,
The human sorrow and smart!
And yet it never was in my soul
To play so ill a part.
But evil is wrought by want of thought
As well as want of heart.

THOMAS HOOD

So let's be thoughtful. We are dealing with sensitive human beings. Be kind! Be kind! Remember—everyone we meet is bearing a heavy burden and fighting a hard battle, and many of them with a weak back and a short stick.

And be ye kind one to another.

EPHESIANS 4:32

Who in our community needs a meal? Who needs a place to live and a few simple clothes for their children? Who needs a friend to listen to the outpourings of their heart? The homeless, the helpless, the hopeless around us are waiting.

You ask about rewards? As we begin to reach out to them, we should see in each one of them the face of our Lord Jesus. Is that not reward enough?

LEROY BROWNLOW

CHAPTER EIGHT

May the Angels Keep Thee

Swing low, sweet chariot,
Comin' for to carry me home;
I looked over Jordan, an' what did I see?
A band of angels coming after me,
Comin' for to carry me home.

OLD SPIRITUAL

Angels guard you when you walk with Me. What
better way could you choose?

FRANCES J. ROBERTS

Men would be angels, angels would be gods.

ALEXANDER POPE

Over all our tears God's rainbow bends,
To all our cries a pitying ear He lends;
Yea, to the feeble sounds of man's lament,
How often have His messengers been sent!

CAROLINE NORTON

If there's anything that keeps the mind open to
angel visits, and repels the ministry to evil, it is a
pure human love.

N. P. WILLIS

Angel voices, ever singing
  Round Thy throne of light;
Angel harps, forever ringing,
  Rest not day nor night.

FRANCIS POTT

Then I looked and heard the voice of many angels,
numbering thousands upon thousands, and ten
thousand times ten thousand.... In a loud voice
they sang:

  "Worthy is the Lamb, who was slain,
   to receive power and wealth and
   wisdom and strength
   and honor and glory and praise!"

REVELATION 5:11-12

To wish to act like angels
while we are still in this
world is nothing but folly.

TERESA OF AVILA

May loving angels guard
   and keep thee,
Ever pure as thou art now.

ANONYMOUS

Angels mean messengers and ministers.
Their function is to execute the plan of divine
providence, even in earthly things.

THOMAS AQUINAS

Stone walls do not a prison make,
   Nor iron bars a cage;
Minds innocent and quiet take
   That for an hermitage;
If I have freedom in my love,
   And in my soul am free,
Angels alone that soar above
   Enjoy such liberty.

RICHARD LOVELACE

Angel Tents

There are who, like the Seer of old,
  Can see the helpers God hath sent,
And how life's rugged mountain side
  Is white with many an angel tent.

They hear the heralds whom our Lord
  Sends down his pathway to prepare;
And light from others hidden shines
  On their high place of faith and prayer.

JOHN GREENLEAF WHITTIER

It's food too fine for angels; yet come take
And eat thy fill! It's Heaven's sugar cake.

EDWARD TAYLOR

When Angels Sing

Hark! the herald angels sing
Glory to the newborn King;
Peace on earth, and mercy mild,
God and sinners reconciled!
Joyful all ye nations rise,
Join the triumph of the skies;
With th' angelic host proclaim
Christ is born in Bethlehem.

CHARLES WESLEY

This world has angels all too few,
And heaven is overflowing.

SAMUEL TAYLOR COLERIDGE

The golden moments in the stream of life rush
past us, and we see nothing but sand; the angels
come to visit us, and we only know them when
they are gone.

GEORGE ELIOT

We trust, in plumed procession,
For such the angels go,
Rank after rank, with even feet
And uniforms of snow.

EMILY DICKINSON

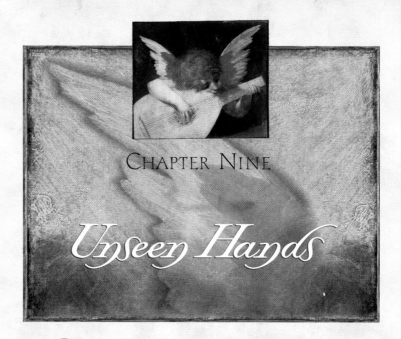

CHAPTER NINE

Unseen Hands

*W*hile angels are employed in a much more humble capacity than the Son of God, they are employed to further the salvation of the people of God, and to assist them in their journey to heaven. In this idea there is nothing absurd. It is no more improbable that angels should help man, than that one person should help another. It is certainly not as improbable as the fact that the Son of God came down "not to be ministered unto, but to minister," and that He performed on earth the office of a servant.

 Indeed, it is a great principle of divine law that one class of God's creatures is to minister to others; that one is to aid another, to assist him in trouble, to provide for him when poor, and to counsel him in storms of doubt. We are constantly deriving benefit from others, and are dependent on their counsel and help. God has appointed parents to aid their children; neighbors to aid neighbors; the rich to aid the poor. And all over the world the principle is seen—that one is to derive benefit from the assistance rendered by others.

Should it be said that angels are invisible, and that it is difficult to conceive how we can be aided by beings we never see, I partly agree. They are unseen. They no longer *appear* as they once did to be the *visible* protectors and defenders of the people of God. But no small part of the assistance which we receive from others comes from unseen sources.

We often owe more to unseen benefactors than to those whom we do see. The most grateful of all aid, perhaps, is that which is furnished by a hand we do not see, and in quarters which we cannot trace. How many an orphan is benefited by some unseen and unknown friend. So it may be a part of the great arrangements of divine Providence that many of the most needed interventions for our welfare should come to us from invisible sources, and be conveyed to us from God by unseen hands.

ALBERT BARNES

CHAPTER TEN

Soft as the Voice of an Angel

The angels in high places
  Who minister to us,
Reflect God's smile, their faces
  Are luminous.

ROBERT GILBERT WALSH

A guardian angel o'er his life presiding,
Doubling his pleasures, and his cares dividing.

SAMUEL ROGERS

Music is well said to be the speech of angels.

THOMAS CARLYLE

Hush, my dear, lie still and slumber.
  Holy angels guard thy bed.
Heavenly blessings without number
  Gently falling on thy head.

ISAAC WATTS

*Like the visitors to the empty tomb, those who are
intent on seeking Jesus will not be satisfied in
finding angels.*

ANONYMOUS

For he will command his angels concerning you
  to guard you in all your ways;
they will lift you up in their hands,
  so that you will not strike your foot
  against a stone.

PSALM 91:11-12

Soft as the Voice of an Angel

Soft as the voice of an angel,
  Breathing a lesson unheard,
Hope with a gentle persuasion
  Whispers her comforting word:
Wait till the darkness is over,
  Wait till the tempest is done,
Hope for the sunshine tomorrow,
  After the shower is gone.

ALICE HAWTHORNE

Remember though thy foes are
* strong and tried,*
The angels of Heaven are on thy side,
* and God is over all!*
ADELAIDE ANNE PROCTER

For adoration all the ranks
Of angels yield eternal thanks.
CHRISTOPHER SMART

Blessed Assurance
Perfect submission,
* perfect delight,*
Visions of rapture now
* burst on my sight;*
Angels descending
* bring from above*
Echoes of mercy,
* whispers of love.*
FANNY CROSBY

It is not because angels are holier than men or
devils that makes them angels, but because they
do not expect holiness from one another,
but from God alone.
WILLIAM BLAKE

Angels, where ere we go,
Attend our steps whate'er betide.
With watchful care their charge attend,
And evil turn aside.

CHARLES WESLEY

The Praise of Angels

After this I looked and there before me was a great multitude that no one could count, from every nation, tribe, people and language, standing before the throne and in front of the Lamb. They were wearing white robes and were holding palm branches in their hands. And they cried out in a loud voice:

> *Salvation belongs to our God,*
> *who sits on the throne,*
> *and to the Lamb.*

All the angels were standing around the throne and around the elders and the four living creatures. They fell down on their faces before the throne and worshiped God, saying:

> *Amen!*
> *Praise and glory*
> *and wisdom and thanks and honor*
> *and power and strength*
> *be to our God for ever and ever.*
> *Amen!*

REVELATION 7:9-12

The angels are the dispensers and administrators
of the divine beneficence toward us; they regard
our safety, undertake our defense, direct our ways,
and exercise a constant solicitude that no evil
befall us.

JOHN CALVIN

For God will deign
To visit oft the dwellings of just men
Delighted, and with frequent intercourse
Thither will send his winged messengers
On errands of supernal grace.

JOHN MILTON

Outside the open window
The morning air is all awash with angels.

RICHARD WILBUR

Jesus replied, "The people of this age marry and
are given in marriage. But those who are consid-
ered worthy of taking part in that age and in the
resurrection from the dead will neither marry nor
be given in marriage, and they can no longer die;
for they are like the angels."

LUKE 20:34-36

All Through the Night

Sleep, my child, and peace attend thee
  All through the night.
Guardian angels God will send thee
  All through the night.

HAROLD EDWIN BOULTON

While shepherds watched their flocks by night,
All seated on the ground,
The angel of the Lord came down,
And glory shone around.

NAHUM TATE

To love for the sake of being loved is human,
but to love for the sake of loving is angelic.

ALPHONSE DE LAMARTINE